# A
# Day
## at the
# Gate

A

# Day

at the

# Gate

by
ED NOWAK

ILLUSTRATIONS BY GINA GUARINO

*Trafford rev. 04/04/2019*

 www.trafford.com

**North America & international**
toll-free: 1 888 232 4444 (USA & Canada)
fax: 812 355 4082

# Dedication & Acknowledgements

To my wife, Janis, who saw very little of me during my paddock master days, my son, Jeff, who was the rider in the family and literally introduced us to the horse show world and my son, Matt, who was dragged to every horse show kicking and screaming, but is a better person for it. And to anyone who gave me a number, volunteered to go first, brought me a Coke and a hamburger, said thank you for anything and might have hinted that maybe all paddock masters are not *&^%$*#.

# Order Of Go

# Forward

When I went public with the idea of writing a book called, "A DAY AT THE GATE," I heard two reactions: The first, from a small minority of the people, said something like, "What a great idea. People won't believe it" and the second was, "Now, there's a book that needs to be written." The majority of my former friends were less than pleased. They said things like. "Forget my name." "Forget you ever knew me." "I'LL SUE!" It was this group that convinced me this book needed to be written.

So, this is for the people in the second group, those whose biggest fear is that someday this book might not only get written, but published. As you page through and see or read something that may seem vaguely familiar, it is purely intentional. Nothing in this book is coincidental. This is not fiction. Everything you see or read in this book actually happened. I mean, who could make this stuff up? Any reference to persons living or dead is absolutely intentional. YOU KNOW WHO YOU ARE!

This book is meant for those horse show people with a sense of humor. It is meant to poke fun and not to make fun. Horse shows are meant to be fun. That is why we go to them, some to work, some to watch and some to exhibit. This is what we do for FUN! (Somebody stop me before I start believing this stuff.)

Horse shows should not be a test of our endurance or an opportunity to add even more stress to our lives. I have seen seven year olds leave a ring and throw up; an adult almost faint from hyperventilating; a parent screaming at her child to "get off the ground; you're not hurt" after the kid's pony refused a fence. A horse show will never cure cancer or solve world peace. It is what most of us do in our "spare" time.

"Fun" should be the operative word. I also recognize, however, that there are those that work very hard to make a living in this very competitive environment. Trainers and show managers, among others, work very hard and survive on the results they produce. Exhibitors spend exhorbatent amounts of money to win a $2.00 ribbon and $1.50 coffee mug. I've been there. I was a horse show parent. I am merely suggesting that from time-to-time we take a deep breath, step back and recognize how fortunate we are to be able to do what we do. As I have told more than one show manager who has been whining around my gate about how its not easy being them, "Just be grateful you do what you do. You could have a real job!" My point is, approach this thing with an ounce of perspective. You could actually have a lot more fun than you think at a horse show

This book is intended to give the reader a snapshot of a day in the life of a paddock master for hunters, equitation and jumpers only. I have no idea what goes on at other types of horse shows. As I said above, this is not fiction. And if I offend anyone because they do not recognize themselves in this book, please be patient. There is enough material at a one day to write three or four books. I'm sure you will do or say something very soon that will get you into print in "A Day At The Gate, The Sequel."

Please have fun with this book. And if you see or hear anything you think I may have missed, tell me the next time you see me. I can only do so much in "a day at the gate."

# You Make The Call

It doesn't really matter what you call him or her. Paddock master, starter, gateman or woman, back gate keeper (west coast), dummy, yutz (everywhere), are just a few of the labels that have been hung on the person that stands at the in-gate with a clipboard and a walkie-talkie and tries to organize the chaos around him. He will respond to all of the above and several other names that can't be printed here. But treat him kindly. (I know respect is too strong a word.) Work with him and he will work with you. He really can make your day a lot less stressful. (TIME OUT. I KNOW THERE ARE PROBABLY AS MANY WOMEN AS MEN THAT WORK AS PADDOCK MASTERS. HOWEVER, FOR THE SAKE

OF BREVITY AND MY SANITY, I WILL REFER TO THE FUNCTION IN THE MASCULINE CASE. IT'S A GUY THING.) I have been told by more than one show manager that paddock master is the most difficult job at a horse show. Show secretary has to be a close second. The reason for this, they say, is because the paddock master and the show secretary are the only two show officials that come into direct contact with everyone on the show grounds, including spectators, from dawn until the last horse leaves the ring and the last entry fee is paid. However, the paddock master deals with exhibitors, trainers, judges, stewards, announcers, parents, grandparents, show managers, the EMT, caterer, et.al. Sometimes all at once. And usually none of these folks is in a great mood. They are either wet or tired, hot or cold, stressed out, hungry or sunburned, and they have a tendency to whine.

IF THERE'S ONE THING THAT CAN MAKE A DAY AT THE GATE LONGER... IT'S **WHINING!**

Therefore, without a good paddock master two things happen and neither one is good: there is chaos at the gate and the show never ends. Now, there are those that might argue that this is always the case, but I like to think not. As you may have noticed, I have a tendency to generalize. I will do so throughout the book. Otherwise, there would be no book. However, if you admit that not all paddock masters are unreasonable, uncaring, ignorant blockheads, I will admit that not all exhibitors and trainers and their connections are self-centered, cranky, whiney, spoiled, inconsiderate, pretentious*&%@#+@.

# Why Me?

People frequently ask me why I work the gate at horse shows. What sin could I have commited that was so grievous that I've been banished to the in-gate for the remainder of time? There are times I ask myself the same question. Like when the rain is coming down so hard I can't see the judge, and the ink on the orders-of-go and course sheets is in a puddle at the bottom of the the course board, and the ribbons are floating past the in-and-out like a wreath thrown from a ship in tribute to classes that won't be run. Or, its 93 degrees in the shade and we haven't even finished warmups yet; or, its so cold I have to tape the pencil to my right index finger just so I know it's there; or, when 25 low hunters have a conflict in the eq. ring. THEN, I might wonder why I do it.

I guess it's a way for me to either revisit or relive the past … kind of like circus folk not being able to get the sawdust out of their veins. Standing at in-gates for 10 or 11 years watching our son show, from 4H to the Garden, will provide a keen sense of what makes a good paddock master. We kept our son's horses at home, shipped them ourselves to lessons and shows, and did our own grooming, except for national finals. Somehow I just couldn't see my wife or me hauling our trailer through Manhattan and sitting on 34th Street all night waiting for the MacClay finals.

IS IT ME OR ARE THINGS JUST DIFFERENT AT THE IN-GATE TODAY?

So, getting started in the paddock master business was not difficult. It all began the year after our son finished his junior career. He was off to college and we had leased his equitation horse. I decided to take a ride to one of the local medal finals to see how the horse was doing. I had barely gotten out of the car when the peripatetic Debby Tate, horse show manager, bon vivant and raconteur approached me.

"Hi, Ed, how've you been?" says Debby. "If I were doing any better, I'd have to go public." (I love saying that.)

"What're you doing with all your spare time now that you're not goin' to horse shows?" says Debby.

"Whatever I want. It's fabulous."

"Wanna help out at some indoor shows this winter?" says she.

Okay. You get the gist. I said I'd love to, figuring she'd never call. WRONG! Next thing I know I'm agreeing to stand at an ingate two days after Thanksgiving in 1989, hanging onto a clipboard and walkie talkie for dear life. This is the first time I ever went to a horse show and didn't bring my check book. They actually gave me a check before I left. What a country! The rest is history. It's kinda like the ole, "Let's get together, give me a call, you bet," kinda thing. WRONG again. Not when you're talking to a show manager. They take everything so seriously. You see, what I didn't know at the time but do today, is that show managers are very desperate people.

AND THEY SAY IT'S HARD TO FIND GOOD HELP TODAY.
(IT'S A JOKE, GUYS)

9

They all need help, badly. They <u>really</u> need good help, but they will take any help they can get. I don't necessarily mean psychological help, although it couldn't hurt.

A show manager will promise you anything just to get you to show up for warmups at 6:30 A.M. They will kill for good, dependable people who have the slightest clue about which end of a horse eats. Although, if you talk to a show manager on the day before a show starts and they have just received a call informing them that three jump crew guys can't make it, they will hire the halt and the lame. They will hire guys on the FBI's ten most wanted list. The TV show, Unsolved Mysteries, checks out horse show grounds before they put the show on the air. Just in case. Why waste air time? Pretty good chance we could find the guy we're looking for chasing rails in the jumper ring.

Getting back to why I do this. There are many more reasons. I love horses. I love and respect the people in the business. They are one-of-a-kind. Of course, there are the occasional pains in the butt you would like to run over, and there are the bad apples that give the industry a blackeye. But every industry has them. We shouldn't feel privileged.

SOME COURSE DESIGNERS CAN TAKE THEIR JOBS JUST A LITTLE TOO SERIOUSLY.

One of the real pleasures, however, is watching the kids and their parents grow and mature, from short stirrup to local medals to the big medals and beyond. For a parent, making the giant step from a pony to a horse is matched only by the look on a parent's face the first time the child does an A.O./

Junior Jumper Class. Most of these kids become solid citizens, sophisticated men and women who will take the life lessons learned from the show experience into their adult lives. I really love seeing that. And it happens more often than not. This is one of the intangibles of spending a day at the gate.

## Warm-ups Or Have You Ever Seen Me Give A Clinic?

First you school and then you warm-up. It doesn't cost anything to school, but it usually costs $10 for the first trip to warm-up and $5 for every additional round. Or sometimes you can buy a ticket for $10 and you can warm-up for 10 minutes, but don't forget to school before you warm-up. It doesn't cost anything.

Why do they call it "warm-ups" anyway? I mean, I always thought that a warm-up was just that. Jump around the 6-8 fence course once, maybe twice, and get out! Where does it say, "Give A Lesson?" I always thought that lessons were given at home in preparation for the show. Silly me. Here they

MAYBE IF WE STARTED WARM-UPS AT 5:30, WE
COULD START THE SHOW ON TIME...YA THINK?

come. Trainer, student, half an hour after they went into the ring, horse dripping with sweat. I ask, in my most politically correct tone, "How many trips?" The trainer looks me straight in the eye and says, without blinking, "One." Who am I to argue?

I know that warm-up classes are a money making proposition for the show management. But try to put down more than three trips on your warm-up sheet and come around three, four o'clock in the afternoon and one of the show secretaries is on the walkie-talkie saying, "Ed ... Ed. Mrs. Alwaysright says her daughter, Tiffany, only did three warm-up rounds. You have her down for four."

IT WAS 10 HOURS AGO! HOW THE HELL DO I KNOW HOW MANY TRIPS MRS. ALWAYSRIGHT'S KID DID?" I CAN'T EVEN REMEMBER IF THERE WAS A WARM-UP! WASN'T THAT YESTERDAY?

I'm trying to find three numbers to complete the Children/Adult Special Hunter Classic and I'm supposed to remember how many trips Tiffany Alwaysright did in the warm-up? Meanwhile, the Alwaysright family has dropped a small fortune in shipping, training and entry fees. No way are they going to get beat out of an extra fiver in warm-up charges. But I digress.

Most shows will give exhibitors one and a half to two hours of warm-up time before the start of the first class. That's at a one day. Most "A" shows provide a full day of warm-ups the day before the show begins. Sounds like plenty of time. No problem. Not so fast, warm-up junkie. Approximately fifteen minutes before warm-ups close and the "last number is taken" by the starter, there will be seven to ten horses standing at the gate begging you not to close the warm-up. Where were these people at 6:30 or 7:00 or 3:00 or an hour before the ring closes? How many think that if we started the warm-ups half an hour earlier or provided an extra warm-up day at the big shows, we could solve the "end of warm-ups" rush? I don't think so. It's just part of the horse show culture.

I GUESS IT'S THOSE ONE TRIP WARM-UPS THAT RENDER THESE ANIMALS UNSOUND BY MEMORIAL DAY.

But here's a suggestion everyone might like, especially horse show managers and warm-up junkies. Set up a ring with an eight fence course. Call it the "Permanent Warm-up Ring". The Permanent Warm-Up Ring opens after the other rings close for warm-ups and the show begins, and it is open ALL DAY. Hire a kid to stand at the gate with a clipboard and count trips, $10 for the first and $5 for every other trip.

I understand that this is not the ring exhibitors will be showing in. It doesn't matter. They have already warmed-up in the rings in which they will be showing. These are warm-up junkies. They won't be able to resist. And they could even take another lesson.

Ever wonder why most horses are sore before Memorial Day?

AND THAT'S HOW THE DAY STARTS. IT'S DOWNHILL FROM THERE.

And here's the corker. It's 5:30 P.M. Ring 1 has 150 trips left. Ring 2 is almost done. The announcer says, "Limit equitation, 12-14 open and National Childrens Medal will be moved from Ring 1 to Ring 2." Before the echo from the P.A. system fades away, 20 hyperventilating trainers rush up to the starter at ring two screaming, "We need a warm-up, we need a warm-up!"

Maybe it's just me. But it seems when my son was riding there was one warm-up at a horse show. And it was early in the morning. If you didn't get to the show in time for the warm-up, you didn't warm-up. Could you just use the open or the low hunter class for a warm-up? But that's only once around. How can you call that a warm-up?

Here are 10 reasons to justify another warm-up (like you need a reason?):

1.  The judge put her umbrella up on the back of the truck. The horses haven't seen the umbrella up.

2.  The jump crew guy moved that bush in on the oxer. The course is different now.

3. The eq kids didn't get to warm-up over 3'. The warm-up this morning was only 2'9".

4. The course designer put a roll-back in the medal course. That wasn't in the warm-up this morning.

5. The judge just put her umbrella down; the horses are confused.

6. The USET course just went up because it just filled. We definitely need a warm-up.

7. It just started raining and the adults haven't jumped in this ring since it got wet.

8. It just stopped raining and the juniors haven't jumped in this ring since it dried out.

9. They moved the outside lines in to avoid the puddles.

10. They didn't move the outside lines in to avoid the puddles.

These just scratch the surface. If you can't think of 10 more you should hand in your USEF card! You're not a real warm-up junkie.

SORRY ABOUT THAT.

# Parents

God love 'um. There are as many parent-types at a horse show as there are exhibitors. Obviously, the older the exhibitor, the fewer the parents. From the mom or dad with a rub rag in their back pocket and a can of hoof oil in their hand to the super yuppie sitting ring-side with a bottle of mineral water and a plate of brie and shrimp. If it weren't for parents there would be no horse show industry. It all starts with the parents. There are those kids that grew up at a barn because their parents are trainers or they rode themselves as kids. But the vast majority come from families that didn't grow up around horses. These are the parents that gave in to the nagging and finally agreed to let the kid take riding lessons. That's when the hook is set and the rest is history.

Of course, if a child rider comes from a family that is, how you say, loaded, then the child has a distinct advantage. He/she can afford the best horses (plural) and training and can go to more and bigger shows. In no way am I implying that these kids don't work as hard as kids from families that are financially challenged. Horse showing is an expensive proposition. It's as simple as that, and the more discretionary income a family has, the more opportunities their child will have to do well in the sport. I often wonder why we never encouraged our son to take up swimming. A Speedo, nose plugs and you're done. (I should have mentioned up front that I also have a tendency to philosophize. If you would rather not plow through this without boots on, just move on and look at the pictures.)

HE MUST BE SO PROUD.

Sometimes I refer to horse showing as "Mom's Little League." This is probably because there are so many more girls than boys riding in the equitation/hunter/jumper divisions. Somewhere along the line girls were given the "horse crazy" gene along with the shopping gene. So, now, mom lives vicariously through her daughter, the rider, not unlike dad and his son, the ballplayer.

And horse show moms can be just as competitive as Little League moms.

I don't know if you have ever sat in the stands at a Little League game or a junior hockey game, but the words that come out of those mothers' mouths would make a Marine blush. Stand at an in-gate for more than five minutes the next time you are at a horse show. "Competitive" is about as nice a way as I can think of to put it. The moms and, yes, some dads, too, aren't actually screaming, "Kill the judge" or other expletives. They would if it weren't considered bad form. However, they aren't too bashful about expressing exactly how they feel about something. And if there are points involved, stand back. "How many were in the National Junior Medal, Ed?" "Ed can you tell me how many were in the Pony Medal? Great that third means one more point and we qualify."

IT'S A MIRACLE THAT ANY OF THESE KIDS MAKE IT OUT OF LEADLINE (OR THE RING!).

Before we leave the parents, I really need to pay tribute to those single parents, and they are usually moms, who will work 15 to 20 hours of overtime each week to pay for next week's show or this week's lesson or a shipping bill or a new pair of boots. These ladies are dedicated, loving and underappreciated. And they usually arrive with the best attitude on the show grounds. They smile a lot and I don't think I have ever heard one of these moms whine. There I go, generalizing again.

All of these moms and horse show parents deserve a "big atta girl" and "atta boy". (Brownies are always appreciated by the paddock master anytime during a day at the ingate.)

THE STARTER CAN BE BRIBED AND WILL PLAY FAVORITES IF GIVEN THE OPPORTUNITY.

# Schooling

"I just have to jump a jump."

Probably one of the biggest lies at a horse show. God did not make one beer, one martini or one jump. I would wager that 90% of the time I ask a trainer if they can go in two, the answer is, "Yah, I just have to jump a jump." And that's the last I see of them until I ask the announcer for a last call. So maybe I exaggerate a little, but not much.

So here's a typical show day in the life of a low hunter. Arrive at the show. Get tacked up. Go to the schooling area. Cross rail, cross rail, vertical, oxer, vertical, oxer, vertical, oxer, etc., etc. etc. Oh, I forgot the 10 minutes of flat work before the vertical, oxer, vertical, oxer, yadda, yadda, yadda. Then it's over to the ring for warm-ups, which in most cases turns into a lesson. So I figure that the average horse jumps at least 40 fences before its first class. Now, this average horse goes in eight classes at a one day show and each class has eight fences. We're up to 104 fences. And if this horse "schools" over a minimum of 10 fences before each of the eight classes, that's another 80 fences. There you have it. This horse has jumped a total of 184 fences, only 64 of which were in the show ring. I think this is a conservative estimate. I also think I have an idea why we have so many sore horses. I was always under the impression that we go to a show to exhibit what we have learned at the farm, and schooling a horse at a show is done to stretch out the horse, and to give the rider an opportunity to get into a rhythm with the horse. But it's 4:00 in the afternoon, 90 degrees in the shade, and the horse is about to go into the ring for the eighth time. But first we have to "jump a jump". Did I mention that we lunged the horse until the his nose touched the ground before we schooled? Just to take the edge off. He was a little fresh when he got off the trailer.

ANOTHER REASON WHY OUR HORSES ARE SORE BEFORE MEMORIAL DAY.

And why is the schooling area always a mile away from the ring?

Trainer: "We're going to school. Let me know when I'm two away."

Starter: "The only way that's going to happen is if you have a cell phone!"

This is usually the case only at the smaller one days. The larger shows load the starter down with enough electronic communications equipment to start a small cable company. Let's see. Channel five talks to the barns. Channel six gets the schooling areas. The announcer for rings one and two is on channel one. The pony ring is on channel three. The EMT is monitoring all channels. Oh, and here's a hailer in case your battery dies. This is also good for getting the ice cream guy. Two more channels and we could qualify for a cable contract and the Horse Show Channel. But the most important thing is you can communicate long distance to the schooling area. Not that anyone is listening. Everybody can know exactly how many away they are. It doesn't matter. They will come to the in-gate when they're ready and not before. Of course, 20 minutes ago you told them they go in three. Now they come over to the gate and are ready to go. You tell them they go in four.

"But you said we go in three!"

"That was 20 minutes ago. I've had eight trips go since you went to school. Now there are three horses lined up and ready to go. You'll be the fourth to go."

The word "idiot" or something that sounds like that is uttered. I've heard it before so I don't take offense.

I need to say to all of those trainers that do not abuse the schooling privilege, that this is not aimed at you. You and I both know who you are and who those other people are.

It's all just another day at the gate.

WE NOW
HAVE SIX
FOR THE
USET!
THE USET
WILL RUN!

33

THIS ACTUALLY HAPPENED.
SIX HORSES IN THE CLASS AND THEY ALL GO TO
SCHOOL AFTER THE COURSE IS SET AND IT'S
GETTING DARK.

# Getting The Show On The Road

Well, we've gotten to the show; we've warmed up; we've schooled, and now it's time to start showing ... I said, it's time to start showing ... I SAID, IT'S TIME TO START SHOWING!

WHY DO I ALWAYS FEEL LIKE I'M TALKING TO MYSELF? I'm sorry. I didn't mean to yell. But, why do I always feel like I'm talking to myself when the time finally arrives to start the show? The only exception to this is if the ring starts with a flat class. Open equitation, 11 years and under. Supposed to have 14 in the class. Looking for five. Going once. Going twice. Going three times. Start the class. The other five race in during the trot to the left. I have also had horses sneak in during the canter the second way of the ring!

"Where have you been?" I ask, rhetorically.

"I didn't know you were ready to staaaaaart," comes the sing-song reply.

It's 8:15. The show is supposed to start at 8:00. Do you think "I didn't know you were ready to start" even deserves a response? I wish I could say this kind of thing is the exception. But it really does happen more often than not. And then the judge looks at me like I'm the idiot that let these five in, and says, "Where the *&#@ did they come from?" Like I'm supposed to know.

The real challenge is to get a ring going at 8:00 with a schooling or special hunter division over fences. To start one show recently, I had 36 special hunters to see twice, and it was raining.

There is little or nothing you can do, short of begging, to speed these folks up on a nice day. (I refuse to beg ... so far.) In the rain it's like being up a creek without a paddle. Literally.

For some reason there is a paranoia in the horse show world about going first in a fences class. Why, I will never know. It starts with a kid's first short stirrup class and it never leaves them for as long as they show. Again, I generalize. It is rarely a problem with professionals, and there are kids, juniors and amateurs who never have a problem with going first. Several volunteer all the time. However, these are the exception. I truly believe it all starts with the trainer. "We have to watch a couple go. But we can go third." Four hunter divisions have been completed. Single; outside line; diagonal; outside line; diagonal. First and second hunter courses almost never change. Approximately 125 trips have been run in the hunter ring. But, we have to watch a couple go first. I always thought it was the exhibitor's responsibility to know the course, know the strides in each line and be ready to go. What do I know?

A PADDOCK MASTER SEES VERY LITTLE OF A HORSE SHOW.

What I do know is there is an unnatural fear of going first. When there is no posted order it is like pulling teeth to get exhibitors to give you their number. If they give you their number they think they are going to have to go first. Not true. Exhibitors and trainers need to understand there is not a professional starter in the business that will force a rider to go into the ring if their trainer is not with them or they are not ready. However, an empty gate or a delay that is unreasonable soon becomes the business of an impatient judge, the show manager and then the show steward. At that point the starter is no longer in control and the steward will close the class, the judge will sign the card and on we go to the next class. It is critical that you give your number to the paddock master. In most cases it is the only way he knows you are in the class, regardless of what the computer sheet says. He will look for you if he is getting toward the end. He does not want to shut you out. But if he doesn't know you are in the class, regardless of what the computer sheet says, he can't look for you. Giving your number to the paddock master does not mean you will have to go first. And please, let him know if you scratch from a class. Just thought I'd mention it.

I have to admit, I believe it is not unreasonable for starters to try almost anything to get a class going. There was the time I was having a heck of a time getting a first horse. A young adult gave me her number but said she would go second. As hard as I tried, I could not find a first horse. So I went over to the girl and said, "Okay. It's your turn."

She said, "I'm going second."

I said, "That's right. It's your turn."

She went into the ring, laid down a perfect trip and won the class.

As it turned out we both got what we wanted. I got a horse in the ring and she got a blue ribbon. I love happy endings.

IS ENGLISH A FOREIGN LANGUAGE AT HORSE SHOWS?

So the key to a happy paddock master and therefore, less stress and more fun for the exhibitor is one word ... communication. Keep the starter informed. He's not a mind reader. He may not like what you tell him, but that's his problem. All of the starters talk to each other via radio. Most of the time it's because they are looking for someone. So talk to us. Ask us to tell the starter at ring one you will be there in two trips. Starters love status reports. They can work around conflicts, but only if they know there is a conflict. And that's how we keep the show on the road.

# (dis)Orders Of (no) Go

There are only two situations when orders of go are helpful: a single ring show where there can be no conflicts and a multi-ring show with big numbers, which allows everyone, in theory, to work around conflicts. It is usually the two or three ring show that is not very big that is the order of go killer. You have seven in your local medal class, three of whom are in the hunter ring when the medal class comes up. Do you wait for the three to come over to your ring when their numbers comes up? Not unless you want to wait to collect social security. You scrap the order of go and try to move the other four through. Hopefully, the three from the hunter ring appear just as the fourth trip goes into the ring. There is a chance, however, they may have to school. There is a roll back in this equitation course, after all.

"ORDERS OF GO" SHOULD BE CALLED "ORDERS OF GO AT YOUR CONVENIENCE"

A rough count shows there are, on average, 16 to 20 classes at a one day that will have orders of go. Count them: three mini medals; USAE Pony Medal; four local medals (two for adults and two for juniors); National Children's Medal; Ariat National Adult Medal; Washington International; two or three classics; USEF Medal; ASPCA Maclay; USET. And at some shows you will find a short stirrup medal and a short stirrup classic. One local show even has a 2'9" classic. And we wonder why these one days can't get finished before dark. It must be that the courses are too long. Yah. That's what it is.

I AM SOOOOO **NOT** GOING FIRST!

SOME KIDS JUST HAVE NO RESPECT FOR AUTHORITY TODAY.

I usually try to have the show office get orders of go to me at least two or three classes before the medal or classic is scheduled, and I ask the announcer to let the folks know the orders are posted. You see, that way it gives the exhibitors plenty of time to plan their schedule so they can be at the gate and ready to go when their number comes up. And if there is anyone out there that actually believes that, I've got a three foot horse for sale that wins on the flat, ribbons at the big shows and is sound; never took a bad step in its life.

So over time you think you have heard just about all of the excuses why someone can't go first. With apologies to David Letterman, here are my

### Top 10 Reasons I Can't Go First

10. I have to wait for my trainer (An ole stand-by; everybody's favorite)

9. I have to school (*Quelle suprese!*)

8. I just got here (I was born at night, but not last night.)

7. I don't know the course. (I've seen you ride; I'm not surprised.)

6. My horse threw a shoe. (I know. I saw him trying to take it off with his teeth.)

5. I lost my number. (Paaleeease)

4. I have to change my bit. (You ought to think about changing your hobby.)

3. I can't find my trainer/jacket/ hard hat/horse – take your pick. (Try Good Will)

2. My parents aren't here yet. (And they're not coming!)

1. Because I never go first. (Until today)

I have to admit that those 10 reasons are pretty common. Most paddock masters hear them every show and more than once. But there is one reason why someone could not go first that I heard once and never heard again.

Here's the scenario: new course is being set, and I'm looking for my first horse in the Adult Medal. Female adult walks up to me and says, "Number 271 is supposed to go first in the medal but she can't."

"Why not?"

Without skipping a beat 271's friend says, "She has cramps."

She has cramps? ... SHE HAS CRAMPS?

I'm about to say something. After all, I feel I should. I always have some sort of a snappy answer for one of the top 10 excuses. But I open my mouth and nothing comes out. I can't think of a thing to say. I've never heard that one before. Just when you think you've heard them all. *She has cramps.* I wanted to applaud. Whether 271 had cramps or she didn't, it doesn't matter. If she did, she gets 10 points for having the guts to be honest. If she didn't, she gets 10 points for creativity. When I stopped sputtering, I asked what seemed to me to be the most logical next question. "Is she going to scratch?" To which number 271's messenger responded, "I'll keep you informed." That's what scared me. My concern was that she would give me much more information than I really needed.

(FYI ... she scratched.)

THE ONLY TIME AT A HORSE SHOW WHEN BEING
FIRST IS NOT A GOOD THING.

# A Paddock Master Is ...

A good paddock master IS all of the following:

- Diplomat
- Priest/Minister/Rabbi
- Mother Theresa
- Ghandi
- A Maitre 'D
- Parent
- The School Principal
- Your Best Friend
- An Electrician
- Underappreciated
- Under Paid

- Always Right

- _____  _____

- _____

I listed just a few attributes of a good paddock master. You fill in the blanks. But, please, be kind.

TO WORK THE GATE AT THE HUNTER RING, IT DOESN'T HURT TO BE A CPA, COMPUTER SCIENTIST, AND/OR PSYCHIC!

A good paddock master is NOT:

- Overpaid
- Ever Wrong
- Over Appreciated
- Your father or mother (He doesn't care.)
- Out to get you
- Freddy Krueger
- A terrorist
- Timothy McVeigh
- Geoffrey Dahmer
- Getting Rich
- On Work Release
- On a career path
- Your clergyman
- _____
- _____

FORMER MAITRE'D'S MAKE EXCELLENT PADDOCK MASTERS.

Okay. Here's your chance. I came up with 13 things a good paddock master, in my estimation, is not. Take your best shot. Fill in the blanks, and again, be kind. And please. This is not a contest. There are no winners. Originality does not count.

But take it from someone that has been on both sides of the gate, exhibitor and paddock master. The gate guy can be your best friend at the horse show. He really can make your life easier. The secret is communication. Keep him informed, and he will really appreciate it. As I said before, he might not like what you tell him, but he will appreciate it. And paddock masters have very long memories. But just remember two other things a paddock master is not. He is not Karnak The Magnificent nor The Amazing Kreskin. He's not a mind reader, although he is probably both magnificent and amazing. (How does he do it?)

Just remember. The paddock master is at the gate in an effort to keep a day at the gate from becoming the longest day at the gate.

WHAT PM LOOKS LIKE TO
EXHIBITORS.

WHAT EXHIBITORS
LOOK LIKE TO PM.

GULP

SOME THINGS ARE JUST NOT IN THE JOB DESCRIPTION.

DO NOT TRY THIS AT HOME!

# Trainers, (Oy!)

Have I given you the impression I have something against trainers? The truth is just the opposite. In my opinion, trainers are the hardest working people in show business. There are two things, however, that separate trainers. One is attitude, and ... actually, I can't really think of another. What it comes down to is attitude. I just figure that how they deal with me is how they deal with everyone: clients, (when did customers become clients?), employees, show personnel, van driver, blacksmith, show secretaries, paddock master. And you can't judge a trainer by the size of his or her barn. There are trainers with the biggest barns on the circuit that are the easiest and most considerate to work with. They operate as professionals in everything they do, which is why they probably have big barns. I have always found in both my business life and my horse show life, it is considerably easier to work with professionals than it is to work with amateurs, and I don't mean the USEF classification of amateur. It doesn't take long to know the status of the individuals with whom you are dealing. It is conceivable that you can have a one horse trainer that can't find his/her way around the show grounds. They are the last ones to warm-up; they are never ready when their client's numbers come up on the order of go; they school the horse or pony until it is about to tie-up and they will argue that the four stride has not been moved out a full foot for the medium ponies.

JUST WHEN YOU THOUGHT THE CLASS WOULDN'T FILL.

The other extreme occurred at a very large "A" show. It was Saturday and the show was running five rings that day: short stirrup, pony, hunter, equitation and jumpers in the derby field. A trainer approached my gate at 7:30 A.M. and informed me he had 19 horses showing that day and would be in all five rings. He was riding five jumpers and had clients showing in all of the remaining four rings. He said he would do his best not to hold me up. I know he went to the other four starters and told them the same thing. Five of his clients were scheduled to show in my ring. Throughout the day he had one assistant, grooms and clients checking with me to see where we stood and asking approximately how long before a particular class would run. The bottom line is he never held up my ring. I never had to wait for him in order to finish a class. When he arrived at the gate, the client was there waiting for him, already schooled and knowing the course. The trainer would ask the rider a few questions, provide a few words of wisdom and into the ring the rider would go. When the rider came out of the ring, the trainer would talk about their round, jump on his bicycle and peddle off to the next ring. But only after informing me how many he had in the next class and where he would be if I needed him. Man, does that make a day at the gate a lot easier no matter how big the show.

A LEARNER PADDOCK MASTER PROGRAM FOR TRAINERS IS SOMETHING THAT NEEDS SERIOUS CONSIDERATION.

Fortunately, there are more trainers like the second example than the first. At least on the circuit I work. As you can imagine, we run into everything in between. But for the most part these men and women work their tails off at a show as well as at the farm: long hours seven days a week with a security factor of zero. There are always exceptions, but for the most part these folks have my respect and admiration for their dedication to the animals and the people that ride them.

I only have three requests for all you trainers that are going to show in my ring: 1. Keep me informed: 2. Tell your clients not to be afraid to give me their numbers, and: 3. DON'T TAKE ALL DAY IN THE SCHOOLING AREA! Schooling is a privilege, not a right.

## Questions, Questions, Questions ... or, someone stop me before I go postal.

They say the only dumb question is the one that is not asked. "THEY" obviously, have never worked a gate at a horse show.

The following questions, in the order of go (not order of questionable question), were asked to me in a 10 minute period at an "A" show, the name and location of which will remain a secret. If we can assume that the average horse show is 10 to 12 hours long, you do the math. Words in parentheses are my own thoughts. There is a big difference between what you can think and what you can say.

1. What time will the mini-medal go?

   (Not soon enough!)

2. How many in the 15-17 fences?

   (More than necessary!)

3. How many left in the 12-14 eq?

   (All of them; it hasn't started, yet.)

4. Is this still the novice eq?

   (God, yes!)

5. How long before limit eq?

   (We call it "limitation")

6. Is there a posted order-of-go for the National Medal?

   (Does it make any difference?!)

7. Do **you** know the course?

   (Why would **I** need to know the course?!)

8. What are the strides in the diagonal?

   (For you it doesn't matter; take my word
   for it!)

9. Why don't you have a classic course posted?

   (Because my goal in life is to make your
   life difficult.)

10. How come I'm not on the order-of-go?

   (They don't want you on it; I'm trying to make your life miserable; I don't even like you! Pick one.)

11. Exhibitor: "How many in the medal?"

   Me: "The order-of-go is posted."

   Exhibitor: "Yah. But how many?

   (Your response here: _____!)

12. I go fifth. Should I get ready?

   (every trainer's favorite question.) or …

   How many do you have lined up? Should I get ready?

   (You'll never be ready!)

13. Is the USET filled?

   (In your dreams!)

14. Is this table two B?

   (Do I look like a maitre'd?!)

15. According to the posted course, there are two fence number nines. Do we do the one that makes sense?

   (If anything makes sense, why are we here?!)

16. Can you move me down?

> (Not far enough!)

17. Do you know what class this is?

> (Excuse me?!)

18. Did they move the lines out? How much?

> (Why did I ever escape from that Turkish prison!)

AND I THOUGHT ONE MEGABYTE OF MEMORY WOULD BE ENOUGH!

I swear. Those questions were asked in 10 minutes. And I have to tell you, some of them were asked more than once! Someday those parenthetical thoughts just might …

I have to (kind of) apologize, however. Not all of the above questions, and many of the others a paddock master is asked during a horse show, are dumb. I understand that there are certain things exhibitors and trainers need to know, and, as luck would have it, the paddock master is the only one with the answers. With this in mind, I'm sure you can understand, why, from time-to-time, your friendly, smiling, happy-go-lucky, not-a-care-in-the-world, everybody's pal paddock master can turn into Freddie Kruegar. Even if for only a brief minute, there is a real good chance the PM, at least once per horse show, will loose it.

LET ME TAKE A WILD GUESS...
THE ONE WITH NO HORSES? NOT!

I know I said that communication is important, so here are a few tips when approaching a starter with what might seem like a perfectly valid question:

If he is chewing his pencil and swallowing the pieces, its not a good time to ask what time the Medal will go.

If it is 3:30 in the afternoon and he has about 150 more trips in his ring, (You know this because you have looked at the course board and counted the numbers on the posted orders of go.) it is probably not a good idea to ask if you should go over to ring three to do your childrens' hunter trips.

If the paddock master has been calling for horses for 10 minutes, and the show management is threatening to close the class (yeah, like that'll happen) and still no horses, it is probably not a good idea to ask him which is the priority ring.

The clock is one minute away from the official sunset time; the show steward is at the gate looking at her watch; the paddock master is trying like crazy to get the Maclay started and you are number one on the order of go. It is probably not a good idea to ask the PM if it's okay to go school.

All of the above apply to other paddock masters. Yours truly, it goes without saying, loves all questions and is always helpful, courteous, kind and understanding.

# Danger Ahead ... (and behind)

I don't think it's a stretch to say that riding horses has an element of risk. There are those that would say it can be down right dangerous. Someone once told me that horses are dangerous at both ends and hard in the middle. That's why the rules insist that hardhats be worn by anyone on a horse anywhere on the show grounds, including in the ring, schooling area or merely sitting on a horse. A few years ago, the rules were amended to state that harnesses be added to the huntcap of all junior riders to keep the hat on the riders head should he or she land on it (head/huntcap). You wonder why rules have to be written to force people to wear a helmet. You would think that common sense … There I go, again, trying to use common sense at a horse show.

YOU NEVER KNOW......

If you think showing can be dangerous from the top of the horse, you ought to try it from where I stand or sit. I could use three more eyes. I need one on the jumping order; one on the on-deck horse; one on the horse in the ring; one on the horse that just came out of the ring, (they always stop in the middle of the gate to discuss their round with their trainer.) and one on the three horses that are either trying to nail me or run me over. This is especially intriguing at a one day indoor show in the middle of winter. You have 54 horses crammed into the space of a good size box stall along with grooms, trainers, parents and grandparents. And, oh yah, me. And for most of these horses, it's the first time out of their own stalls since Thanksgiving. This is another example of trying to put three pounds of you-know-what into a two pound bag.

NEVER TURN YOUR BACK ON A NOVICE EQUITATION FLAT CLASS, OR ANY FLAT CLASS FOR THAT MATTER!

I have come to realize that you cannot find a safe place on a show grounds. This is particularly true in the secretary's office, but that's another story. You can never relax. Here are a number of suggestions to keep you and your loved ones safe at a horse show:

The stable area is a zoo. There is never a good reason to go there.

- Stay away from the trailer area in the morning when they are unloading and in the afternoon when they are loading. And never park your car there.

- You can be run over while standing in the middle of the ring calling a flat class.

- Never walk behind a horse, or particularly a pony, when you have the option of walking in front of it. ("Oh, he won't kick," says the kid on the pony's back, as the animal's ears are pinned flat against his head, and his eyes are the size of baseballs.)

- Never park your car where there is the slightest chance it can be kicked. To be safe, leave it at the hotel and take a cab.

- Jack Russells and Corgies cannot be trusted, particularly if you are eating French Fries.
- Never try to stop or catch a runaway horse; that's why we have jump crews

  Hint: Standing directly in the path of a loose horse waving your arms **only works some of the time.**
- Never loose sight of the EMT.

AND I'M FROM THE GOVERNMENT AND I'M HERE TO HELP YOU!

IF THAT WERE TRUE, THEY WOULDN'T HAVE TO CHARGE ENTRY FEES.

# Priorities

Why is it I get the feeling that the number one prioirity of the majority of horse show exhibitors is not to show at all. They love going to horse shows. Heck, they pay through the nose for the privilege. It's the going in the ring and showing part they're not too crazy about. They love shipping in, seeing all their friends, going out to dinner, warming up and schooling. Oh, how they love schooling. Catching up on all the horse show gossip is also a major priority. But when it's time to show, the excuses are classic. The three most overused excuses have to be: trainer conflict; I have to school; and the ever popular, I don't know the course. Five hunter divisions have already been run in this ring and we're doing the first hunter course, WHICH NEVER CHANGES. Does single, outside, diagonal, outside, diagonal sound familiar? But I digress.

RULE #1 - THE ROAD TO THE MEDAL FINALS IS OVER THE PADDOCK MASTER.

Just once I would love to hear, "Hey, Ed. I'm in this class, but I also have to get over to the equitation ring. Can I get in and do my two hunter courses soon before I go over to the other ring? And I don't have to school. I'm ready NOW." Now, there's an exhibitor with his priorities in order. He actually came to the show to show his horse(s). Okay, there are people out there that operate like that, and I know who you are. I appreciate everything you do to make my job easier. But believe me, you guys are in the minority. You have no idea what it is like to try to get a ring going and keep it going and have an exhibitor sitting on a horse staring at you like you have two heads when you ask if they are in this class, and there is no one else in sight, and you have 27 in the class. And the exhibitor finally works up the courage to speak and says, "No, I'm not."

A HORSE SHOW EMT CAN BE A REAL LIFESAVER!

Maybe someday, if I can ever figure out the priorities of the average horse show exhibitor, a day at the gate will become a little less stressful.

IT REALLY WORKS....

# Judges

I've taken shots at just about everyone on the show grounds – trainers, exhibitors, show managers, secretaries, parents and jump crew. There is no way I can ignore judges. I spend so much time with my back to the ring looking for horses, I really can't tell a good judge from a bad one. I suppose I could listen to what goes on around me. There is no shortage of opinions around the gate. Somehow, I don't think these people are totally objective. I'm not sure you can believe things like, "She must be on drugs." "What ring was he watching?" And then there is the ever popular, "This judge sucks!" On the other hand, you wouldn't believe some of the things I've heard a judge say about a horse, rider, class or an entire show. That's because the person sitting on the other side of the ring in the back of a pickup truck or under a tent is a very opinionated person. They have to be. Why else would they be a judge? And he or she even gets paid for their opinion. They know what they like and don't like and use horses accordingly. I once heard someone say that when you go to a horse show, you are paying for someone else's opinion. The problem seems that very few people, other than the winner, agree with the only opinion that really counts.

IF I WANT TO MAKE CONVERSATION?
IF I WANT TO MAKE CONVERSATION?
THERE IS NO WAY I CAN MAKE THIS STUFF UP!

On the other hand, I have run across some pretty funny judges. I guess you need a sense of humor to sit in the hot sun all day watching nine million hunters jump the same two courses all day.

Like the time a low hunter had three refusals and was excused from the ring. The rider started to wail-away on her horse in the middle of the ring. From my radio I hear, "Ayeydddd. (Some people can turn Ed into a five syllable word.) If you would like to make conversation with her, she can only hit her horse a couple of times." They have such a nice way of putting things in the South, don't they? If that had been a judge from, say, one of the northeastern states, the voice over the radio might have gone something like this: **'Ed. Tell that \*&%$#\* when she gets off her horse to get her a-- over here. And call the steward. I want to talk to her.'** Ya think?

Then there was the time we were running out of daylight. We had just finished the Medal and the judge had barely finished the test and pinning the class. We have six for the

MacClay, and I tell the first rider to get her butt in the ring. We run six through, and it's so dark I can hardly see the judge on the other side of the ring. The sixth horse finishes the course and I'm running across the ring to the judge to do the flat phase. I get to the judge. She looks me right in the eye and says, "What class did I just judge?" "The MacClay, "I said, "and it's not over. If you look real hard, you will see six horses going in a circle."

Or how about the time a judge at an "A" show spent more time talking to spectators, exhibitors and trainers than he did watching the class. The show manager tried everything possible to separate the judge from the public. Pony ring, hunter, equitation … nothing seemed to work. The judge always seemed to be in a position where he could chat with passersby. Then someone came up with a brilliant idea. The next morning, all three judges arrive at the show to find a pick-up truck parked in the middle of the equitation ring. An umbrella is perched on the back of the truck and the fences are set around the truck like an obstacle course. The show manager approached the judge in question. As she examined the top of her sneakers, she handed him a clipboard and a radio and said faster than that fast talker guy who used to do the Federal Express commercials, "(Name omitted to protect the judge and the show manager.), you'll be in that ring today," pointing to the lovely center piece in the middle of the equitation ring. To avoid having to answer questions from the exiled judge, the show manager turned on her heels to start talking to anyone. Unfortunately, everyone, including starters, jump crew, secretaries, announcer and the other judges had abandoned ship. There she was, under the big top, one-on-one with the naughty judge. I'm not sure what they said to each other (I was the first rat to desert), but the judge did sit in the middle of the ring, the show got done and everyone, except you-know-who, was happy.

WITH ALL DUE APOLOGIES TO JIMMY LEE, THIS
ACTUALLY DID HAPPEN.
I'LL NEVER TELL WHO SAID IT.

This last story was told to me by a judge. It seems he was judging a lead-line class. After having each kid walk, trot, etc. both ways of the ring, he asked the class to line up at one end of the ring so he could ask each kid a question.

"What color is your pony?" was the question.

He went from kid to kid and received the appropriate answer. That is, until he reached the last exhibitor in line.

"What color is your pony?" asked the judge.

The young man, who couldn't have been more than five years old, raised himself as tall as he could in the saddle, and without hesitation, said, "Brown." The judge looked puzzled, since the young, self-confident equestrian was obviously sitting on a gray pony.

"Are you sure?" questioned the judge.

"Yup," said the boy.

"But this pony is gray," said the judge.

With all the self-assurance in the world, the future Olympian responded, "This isn't my pony!"

You'll never guess who won the class!

No one will ever agree with how a judge pins every class. But when you consider the number of horses he or she sees at a typical show, it's amazing what they do. It's no wonder the USEF makes it difficult for a potential judges to get their card. It takes a special kind of person to become a horse show judge. I'm sure as hell not one of them.

# And Then ... There's More

Just when you think it's over. Just when you think there is nothing more to say about a day at the gate, something happens that just can't be ignored. Will the comedy never end?

There are dozens of things that happen at a horse show that don't fit neatly into any particular category or under a specific heading other than, "You Must Be Kidding!" As I said early on in this rant, this is real stuff. None of it is made up, fabrication, fiction or a figment of my imagination. I'm really not that clever.

Here's an example. We'll call it, "This Little Piggy Went To A Horse Show."

Every summer there are a number of horse shows on Cape Cod. What better place for a horse show? Gentle breezes, sun, surf, seafood, sand dunes and salty air. Bring the kids, grandma, grandpa and the family Jack Russell. Grab the beach umbrella, the sun block and the boogie board, and don't forget the horse. During one two week stretch, there were two "A" shows in Buzzards Bay. The show management works extra hard to not only put on quality horse shows but to provide exhibitors with every opportunity to enjoy some of the wonderful things the Cape has to offer during the summer months. In the past they have organized deep sea fishing trips, whale watches and evening cruises through the Cape Cod Canal, from Buzzards Bay to Cape Cod Bay. And each week they even put on a real Cape Cod clam and lobster bake. One year they decided that, since many of the exhibitors stayed for both weeks, they would change things up the second week and offer a pig roast instead of a clam bake. (Not very Cape Cod, but what the hell. It's a long summer.)

Early in the morning on the day the pig thing was scheduled, the pigman arrived to begin the cooking and roasting and smoking process. After all, a good pig roast cannot be rushed. What seemed like the logical place for the pigman to set up shop was right next to the exhibitors' tent, where the feast would take place later that evening. You should know that the exhibitors' tent was located on one long side of the ring with the ingate directly opposite on the other side of the ring. Pigman was very considerate and waited for the class in the "pig ring" (as it became known) to end before he moved his roasting/smoking contraption into place. This contraption, which could have doubled as a third world space shuttle, was pulled by a pickup truck and resembled a box about six feet square with doors on the back and a chimney sticking out of the top. With the pig thing in place, the next class began. I think it was an amateur owner/junior jumper deal. I am doing what I normally do at this stage, which is to turn my back on the ring (there is obviously nothing going on there. It's the beginning of a new class!) to find, cajole, encourage and threaten exhibitors to get the class started. So, what I didn't see was pigman take the unfortunate object of the roast from his pickup and place it on the tailgate of the truck. When I turned around I saw a pig, large enough to feed a small country, on its back. The guy had a knife that looked like it could have been a war souvenir, ready to begin pig surgery. It wasn't long before he started pulling "things" out of the pig.

Since I stood about 100' away from the operating theater and it had been years since I had witnessed a pigectomy, I could only identify the items exiting the pig as "things." And the way this guy was having at it, I was sure he wasn't a moehl. At this point, the class had started. The course called for the rider to go across the diagonal on the left lead, take a right turn at the end of the ring and jump the line that went in front of the judge, until now known as the "judges line." (You know, "How many strides in the judges line?") The pig surgeon had already stoked up the smoker, so there were copious amounts of smoke and strange smells coming from the little chimney as he continued to operate on the pig. (As it turns out, the pig was, mercifully, already dead before it got to the show grounds.)

THIS LITTLE PIGGY WENT TO A HORSE SHOW....

As the first horse made the right hand turn at the end of the ring and headed toward the outside line, the sun flashing off the pig surgeon's knife blade got the attention of the big gray gelding. He immediately darted to the right and wanted nothing to do with that particular piece of real estate. The rider circled and tried again. Same result. Mind you, the horse is stopping at least five strides away from the fence. The pig-man is hard at work and, of course, unaware that his presence and actions are having a dramatic effect on the real reason we are even there, the horse show.

Meanwhile, there is panic at the gate. I am surrounded by at least nine or ten people ... exhibitors, spectators, jump crew, who are just beginning to comprehend what is happening. I have the next two horses to show lined up. (Every once in a while I get lucky.)

The rider sitting on the on-deck horse is ashen. Her mouth is wide open, but words fail her. Her eyes are like lasers, staring across the ring at a sight she cannot comprehend. A girl, about 12, is standing next to me and breaks the silence by asking the rhetorical question, directed at no one in particular, "What is that man doing over there?" A groom screams as if she is witnessing pigacide, "My, god. He's killing that pig!" At which point there is a cacophony of "Oh mygodWhat'shedoingNowayI'mdoingthisclassI'mscratching

CallmymotherCallthepoliceCalltheEMT" and many other half intelligible rants.

Across the ring, pigman, who has worked up quite a sweat in the 90 degree heat, is up to his elbows in the pig, proper seasoning being the secret to great pig. The chimney on the smoker/roaster is belching smoke as if we had just elected a new Pope and odors, foreign to most of us, ride a west wind across the ring and through the stable tents. About this time, the rider on the big gray gelding realized the reason her horse was more disobedient than usual and made a sharp right turn and galloped to the outgate. This is the point at which I picked up my radio and said, "Houston, we have a problem."

As you can imagine, the show in ring one came to a screeching halt. Show management convened an impromptu meeting, department heads, only. The show manager, along with the EMT, (Hey, the guy had a knife!) made the long walk to the operating theater. They stood huddled about five feet behind the crazed pig butcher, trying to time their final approach as to not become part of the pig feast later that night.

The man, who I am sure considered himself the Rodney Jenkins of the pig roasting business, had worked himself into an absolute spell and was totally unaware of the havoc he had created. He did not appreciate being interrupted. After all, what artist likes to be interrupted just when his performance is reaching its final crescendo? After explaining the reality of the situation, the pigman, although not happy, acquiesced and agreed to stop the process long enough to move his operation to a location more conducive to roasting a pig at a horse show.

The show resumed in the Pig Ring, as it became known for the rest of the week. The big gray gelding, along with his rider, had time to regain their composure and were given another opportunity to jump the course, which they did, but not before the horse took a real close look at the spot where he had seen a pigectomy in progress. I think this is probably the strangest thing, among a whole lot of strange things, I have ever seen happen at a horse show. And I guess I have to concede, that was probably one of the few times it was not a good idea to go first. But as I stated earlier, just when you think you have seen it all …

# Writing To Conclude

It takes so many hard working people to put on a successful horse show, regardless of the size. From the smallest one day, backyard show to the biggest "A" show or grand prix, it takes dedicated, hard working, knowledgeable people. The guy at the gate is only one of many responsible for the success or failure of a horse show. The show manager, steward, secretary(s), announcer, judges, jump and ring crew, EMT, caterer, grounds keeper, the guy that drags the ring and, of course, the exhibitors, all contribute to determining how successful or unsuccessful show is. You always remember the shows that are well run, and those are the ones you plan to return to year after year. My view of a horse show from the ingate is myopic, to be sure. However, if you are reading this, you have probably read everything that preceded it or at least looked at the cartoons. I think you will have to admit that some pretty weird stuff happens in a day at the gate. I mean, do you think a judge or show secretary has this much fun? Maybe I shouldn't really call it fun. It's more like entertainment without the cover charge. You need to keep in mind that a horse show never cured cancer, and a horse show will never bring about world peace. So if you can't have fun at a horse show, why would anyone spend 12 to 14 hours freezing, drowning or sweating at an ingate? It must be the money. Ya think? To do that you really have to be a masochist. I might be a lot of things, but that is not one of them.

As the years begin to take their toll, I am starting to cut back on the number of shows I work, at least at the gate. At my tender age, I am beginning a new show career – ringmaster. Yes, I have the horn, the flashy red jacket and the top hat. So if you don't see me at the gate, I'll still be around the show, watching, listening and taking notes. There could be a sequel.

Before I crawl back to the gate, I really have to thank the people most responsible for making this book possible. The exhibitors, parents, trainers, grooms, jump crew, judges, show secretaries, show managers and anyone that appears at my in-gate during a horse show. Without you there would be no day at the gate. Writing to conclude, I'll see you at the next show.

Elaine, is the USET filled?

## About the Author

Ed Nowak has spent 15 years working in-gates at horse shows in the Northeast. His son, Jeff, rode hunters, jumpers and equitation for eight years, which introduced Ed to the wonderful, wacky and oftimes whimsical world of horse shows. He also works as the ringmaster at many of the medal finals in and around New England. For 15 years Ed played polo and currently breeds and races Strandardbreds. When not at a horse show or the race track, he owns and operates an advertising and public relations agency in Providence, RI.

Printed in the United States
By Bookmasters